Going to the Market

by Jeanne Tao

Illustrated by Jaime Zollars

Editorial Offices: Glenview, Illinois • Parsippany, New Jersey • New York, New York
Sales Offices: Needham, Massachusetts • Duluth, Georgia • Glenview, Illinois
Coppell, Texas • Sacramento, California • Mesa, Arizona

"Lisa," said Mama, "I need you to do some errands."

"Can I go?" asked Jenny.

"What would you do?" Lisa asked Jenny.

"I can help carry bundles," said Jenny.

"Yes, you may go," said Mama. "Lisa, here is a list of foods to buy at the market. Girls, help each other."

"This is a long list," said Lisa. "We have a lot of food to buy."

"What will we buy first?" asked Jenny.

"We'll go to get curry," said Lisa.

"What is curry?" asked Jenny.

"Curry is a spice," said Lisa. "Mama uses curry when she cooks."

"Good morning, girls," said Mr. Sharma.
"How can I help you?"
"We would like some curry," said Lisa.
"Curry? I have lots of curry," said Mr. Sharma.
He took a box of curry from the shelf.
Lisa took the money out. She paid.
Then the girls said good-bye.

"What is next on the list?" asked Jenny.

"Tomatoes," said Lisa. "We'll go to the outdoor market for tomatoes. Mrs. Rios has a vegetable stand there."

"What is a vegetable stand?" asked Jenny.

"A vegetable stand is a place where someone sells vegetables," Lisa answered.

The girls walked through the market to Mrs. Rios's stand.

"Good morning, girls," said Mrs. Rios. "How can I help you?"

"We would like some tomatoes," said Lisa.

"Tomatoes? They are right here," said Mrs. Rios. She helped the girls pick out three red tomatoes. She put them in a bag.

Lisa paid Mrs. Rios. Then Lisa took the bag and handed it to Jenny. The girls said good-bye.

"What is next on the list?" asked Jenny.

"Fish," said Lisa. "Mr. Li has a fish stand here in the market. We always buy fish from Mr. Li."

"I love fish," said Jenny.

"I know that," said Lisa. "I'll let you carry the fish, too."

"Lisa, it's good to see you," said Mr. Li. "What can I do for you girls today?"

"We would like some fish," said Lisa.

"Fish? I have lots of fish," said Mr. Li.

Lisa pointed to a big fish. Mr. Li picked it up. He wrapped it in paper and put it in a bag. He handed the bag to Lisa. Lisa handed the bag to Jenny.

Lisa paid Mr. Li for the fresh fish. Then the girls waved good-bye.

"What is next on the list?" asked Jenny.

"It's parsley," said Lisa. "But I can't remember what parsley is."

"I know what parsley is," said Jenny. "It's a small, green plant with curly leaves. Mama uses parsley when she cooks."

"Did you see any parsley in the market?" asks Lisa.

"No," said Jenny. "It is one thing on the list we won't be able to buy here."

On their way home, the girls saw their neighbor, Mrs. Jones, in her yard.

"Good morning, girls," said Mrs. Jones. "I see you have been doing errands. You are carrying a lot of packages, Jenny."

"Yes," said Lisa. "We bought a lot. But we couldn't find parsley at the market."

"Parsley?" said Mrs. Jones. "I have some parsley in my garden."

parsley

"That small green plant is parsley," said Mrs. Jones. "I'll cut some for you."

Mrs. Jones put the parsley in a bag and handed it to Lisa. Lisa handed it to Jenny.

"Thank you so much!" said Lisa.

"Lisa," said Mrs. Jones. "Jenny is carrying all the bundles. Don't you think you should help?"

"Oh!" said Lisa, "I'm sorry, Jenny. Give me two of those bundles!"

The girls walked home.

"Did you get everything?" asked Mama.

"Yes, we got everything," said Lisa, "even the parsley."

"Did you help carry some of the bundles, Jenny?" asked Mama.

"No," said Jenny. "I carried ALL of the bundles to our street!"